MOMS NEVER Stop Momming

AND WE COULDN'T IF WE TRIED
(ESSAYS ON PARENTING TEENS AND BEYOND)

Esther Joy Goetz
Melissa Faith Neeb

Copyright @2023 by Esther Joy Goetz and Melissa Faith Neeb, Authors.

All rights reserved. No part of this publication may be reproduced, stored in a retrieval system, or transmitted in any form or means - electronic, mechanical, photocopy, recording, or any other - except for brief quotations in printed reviews, without the prior permission of the Authors.

Unauthorized use of this work may infringe upon the Authors' rights and could result in legal action.

Printed in the United States of America.
First edition.

To our people.

Our partners.

Our kids.

Our friends.

Our writing community.

And especially to each other.

We are ever so grateful.

Esther & Melissa

TABLE OF CONTENTS

ABOUT THE AUTHORS

1 HIS VERY FIRST CALL
2 A YEAR LEFT
3 NERVOUS WRECK
4 DOCTOR'S OFFICE
5 PERMISSION

6 STILL BECOMING
7 TWO SPOONS
8 NOT READY
9 ON LEAVING THE NEST
10 GOOD MOM

11 I'D RATHER
12 MARTYRS
13 SAFE
14 THE THING
15 NOT.A.DARN.THING.

16 THE BATHROOM STALL
17 WILD HORSES
18 A THOUSAND SUNRISES
19 TEARS
20 A PILE OF JOY

21	THE VOW
22	UNTIL HE WASN'T
23	PAPER CHAINS
24	I KNOW YOU
25	FLY
26	AN OPEN LETTER
27	Y-E-S
28	CLOSED DOOR
29	LITTLE BROWN BAG
30	HARD THING
31	QUITTING
32	GLITTER
33	LET THEM LEAD
34	GRIEVE
35	DROPPING SHOES
36	NOTHING DAYS
37	MESSES
38	SHOW UP
39	PRESENCE
40	DON'T KNOW

41 TWINGE
42 THE DRESS
43 CAR ACCIDENT FUND
44 SENIOR
45 HERS

46 SLEEPLESS
47 FIXING
48 LIMIT
49 GOODBYES AND HELLOS
50 MORE TIME

ACKNOWLEDGEMENTS

ABOUT THE AUTHORS

MEET ESTHER

Someone once asked me what the hardest stage of parenting is and I responded, "teens and up." Then they asked me what my favorite stage of parenting is and I also said "teens and up."

As a mom who is smack dab (and always will be) in the middle of this stage of parenting my four budding adults, I've learned that there are two things that I have I've held onto with every fiber of my mom being: give our kids the roots of unconditional love and the wings of freedom to be completely themselves.

Sounds lofty and impossible, but it is actually grounding and simple.

Since having four kids means also having all that goes along with navigating the tricky tightrope of individual needs, family dynamics, the push/pull of the holding on and letting go years, and the weight of what the world "out there" shouts in all of our ears, I have found these two principles to be a lifeline, a huge source to building a healthy, long-lasting relationship with my kids, something that I've wanted since I saw those two lines on my pregnancy test.

Lest you think I've got it all together now and everything is just ponies and rainbows, I don't and it's not.

It's been a long, slow journey for this mom who completely fell apart in her late-30s because, once I had kids and especially when they hit the teen years, I found out that I did not have it all under control and that was scary, and to be honest, downright terrifying.

I wanted good kids. I wanted a good family. I wanted everyone to make good choices, especially my teens (because, you know). I wanted a good life. Period.

But what I learned and keep learning (even after three decades) is this: it's more important to have love than to have perfection.

It's more important to have love than to have all my ducks in a row. It's more important to have love than to have no conflict.

Because love is true and real and raw and vulnerable and healing and beautiful and sacred and where life is full of the messy, gorgeous parts where two (or six in our case) people can come together and receive grace for who we have been and are now and space for who we will be and are becoming.

Buckle up, my friends. You are in for some tears and some laughs, perhaps a "me too" and maybe a "glad that's not me," but mostly, you are in the real, the raw, the brutal and the beautiful, and ultimately, the wild hope that is motherhood.

MEET MELISSA

No one could have prepared me for how much I would love this season of parenting.

The other seasons of their childhood, I knew. I knew how awesome it was to see their little personalities develop, how much I adored their need for me (even though it was completely exhausting most of the time), and that I had plenty of time left with them.

But now, there is so much less.

Between hibernating in their rooms, always having earbuds in on car rides, one off to college and the other one soon to be, I am deep in the thick of both grieving the endings and cherishing what's left.

What a privilege it is to witness their lives: all the messy, all the glory of it.

I was prepared, as much as I could be, for how hard it would be. The mood swings and slammed doors, the isolating and the eye rolls. All of that I remember from my own angsty teenhood.

I was prepared for the sleepless nights and the constant worry, the midnight phone calls and the fierce knots of anxiety.

But no one told me about the way my heart would rejoice every time they asked for my advice on a hard thing they were navigating through, or how watching their eyes light up doing what they loved would make me weep with joy.

No one mentioned how good the relationship would get as it transformed from parent/child to friendship. The deep conversations we would have long into the night. The day trips we would take to anywhere, with the music cranked and the laughter flowing. The ordinary moments of being in each other's presence. The gift of that.

The teen and young adult years have me holding the tension of desperately yearning for the littles they once were to being so grateful to watch them be who they've been becoming all along.

What I hope that I've forged with my kids is a safe place for them to land, a home they always want to come back to, a person they never have to put on masks for, and a lifelong friendship that is just getting started.

Sometimes loving our kids means letting them go when all we want to do is hold on tighter.

MOMS OF BIGS
estherjoygoetz.com

1
HIS VERY FIRST CALL

"Mom, I got bad news totally out of the blue."

The text flashes across my screen.

"You free?"

My heart starts to pound. My hands get sweaty.

"Yes." I respond, gathering my nervous self together as humanly possible.

It feels like hours until the phone rings.

"Is he hurt?"
"Did his girlfriend break up with him?"
"What about his job?"
"Has he been arrested?"

All those crazy (but somehow normal) mom thoughts fly at me from all directions, the "I-WANT-HIM-TO-BE-OKAY" mom thoughts.

My phone finally buzzes.

"Hey honey, what's up?" I ask, hoping I sound calm and not like I'm gripping the side of the chair ready to hear the worst news ever.

He talks to me about what's happening.
I try to just listen.

He tells me how he really feels.
Now, I lean in quieter and harder, because this is a newer thing he's comfortable sharing.

As we get to the end of the call, he thanks me for my support and says, "I love you, Mom."

"I love you, too, honey." I answer. "It's all going to be okay. You will be okay."

I press the red hang-up button.
Tears well and come tumbling out.

But not for the reasons I thought they would.

They are not there because of the sad and hard that my son is experiencing, even though I feel all those same feels.

They spill out because of the gratitude that seeps into my soul, knowing that I am his very first call.

His very first call.
The way I want it to be.

His very first call.
My mama heart rests peacefully.

[Esther]

2
A YEAR LEFT

I have a year left with you, and I feel it.

These next few months will be full of decisions for you, decisions that will take you away from me.

They will be also full of lasts. Last first day of high school. Last homecoming. Last ski race. Last awards banquet.

There will be senior prom and graduation and a graduation party.
But it is not the big moments or rites of passage that I'm going to miss the most.

It's the everyday.

The "Morning mom," and "Bye mom."

The long discussions about your crushes as you straighten your hair and I sprawl on your bed.

The scent of your favorite perfume lingering in your room long after you've left.

Borrowing your shoes. You have good ones.

Hearing your high-pitched giggle when you are talking to your bestie.

Peeking in and watching you sleep so angelically. So peacefully. With the lump of a dog under your blanket and your arm around a cat.

The moments we are in the same orbit are getting rarer.

Your roots deepen, your limbs stretch to the sky.

As I long to get closer, you move further away. It is the natural order of things.

Darling, I don't know how to do this. This slow goodbye.

I take every snippet of time I can get.

Long talks and coffee dates. Day trips and weekend getaways.

Late-at-night laughing and afternoons at the lake.

Saturday afternoons thrifting and grocery store runs for ice cream.

Lounging together on your bed watching videos on your phone.

I love you so much.

So if I hold on a little too long, sweet girl,
Let me.

[Melissa]

3
NERVOUS WRECK

Once upon a time, there was a mom who was a nervous wreck.

She didn't quite know what to do.

She wanted to have "the talk."

Not the one about the birds and the bees.
Not the one about just saying no.
Not the one about the future.

It was a completely different, way more nuanced and complicated talk.

The kind that might make her big kid defensive.
Or shut her out.

The kind where she went through all the scenarios in her head.

When should she do it?
How should approach the subject?

What should she say?
This or that or the other thing?

Her mind raced and looped and her stomach got all knotty inside.

She loved this big kid so desperately.

She worked so hard to keep her mouth shut and opinions to herself.

She did not want to do anything that would hurt this kid or their relationship.

But this was one of those times when talking was really important.

It couldn't and shouldn't be swept under that rug where the pile grows into a huge bump that no one can get over or around.

This was one of those times when talking was scary, but oh so necessary and really good.

For her big kid.
And for herself.

She got up the gumption after a few nervous-nelly days to say, "Can we take a walk just by ourselves?"

When the answer was "I'd love to Mom," she said a little prayer for help, mustered up her brave mom heart, put on her cute white shoes and took the first step out the door and into what might end up horrible or wonderful.

At first, she asked lots of questions that had nothing to do with anything about anything.

She was hoping to make it feel like she didn't have this weird mom agenda about to pounce.

Next, she talked about all the beautiful sights on the walk, the tulip trees in bloom and how the neighbor had shaved her dog in the strangest of ways.

She was avoiding.

Finally, in the most normal, not awkward mom way she possibly could, she carefully tiptoed her way into "the talk."

She tried so hard not to "set her big kid straight."
She tried so hard to listen and understand.
She tried so hard to share her thoughts and concerns from a place of love and not fear.

And guess what?
It went better than she could have imagined.

What could have gone sideways, upside-down or completely backwards went mostly straight.

What could have ended in tears, slammed doors and broken hearts ended in a hug.

It wasn't because this mom did it all perfectly. That's not true, not true at all.

This mom actually has no idea why it went so well.

Maybe it was because they had slept well and eaten a good breakfast.

Maybe it was because they just loved each other and had worked really hard to do these kinds of talks better than they had done a million other times.

Maybe it was none of those things.

Who really knows?

But this mom does know a few things right now.

She can take a deep breath and her tummy can unknot.
She will offer a huge prayer of thanks.

She is not a nervous-wreck mom anymore. She is a glad one.

[Esther]

4
DOCTOR'S OFFICE

I sat in a doctor's office once with my teen and heard unexpected words spilling out of his mouth, spilling like milk all over the floor, splattering on my toes and exploding all over my thoughts.

I knew a fraction.
Just the tiniest fraction.

How had I missed this? How had I walked right by the signs with blazing arrows and gone a different way?

The doctor asked if these words surprised me and if there ever was a dumb question, that would've been it. Surprise was confetti-ed all over my face. But this was no party.

This was horror.

My precious baby was saying words from the English language that were impossible, incomprehensible.

I couldn't arrange them to fit in my brain. I crossed my legs and tried to appear calm while a hurricane raged within.

As my terror rose, his limbs and face visibly relaxed.

Clearly he was exhausted from carrying this, and expelling it into the universe and into this exam room was the correct dose of the exact right medicine.

I felt the walls morph and shrink; I think he felt them blow off the foundation.

But we were there, in that space of simultaneous shrinking and exploding, together.

We discussed options and formulated a plan.

In that moment, neither of us were okay, yet somehow we were more okay than we had been in a long time.

The truth of things does that.

It makes us feel worse and better and terrified and relieved and helps us move forward, move past the shadows and shame, tiptoe steadily, shakily forward.

And sitting in both the darkness and the light are better when we have the warmth of each other in the next chair while we wait.

[Melissa]

5
PERMISSION

It was one of those HIGHLY stressful mornings where nothing went right.

Certain people had forgotten their uniform when they rushed out the door after scarfing down a protein bar (aka, my high school junior).

Other people had texted, freaking out that they overslept and were late to their final exam (aka, my college sophomore).

Still other people had written in ALL CAPS about being responsible and how did this happen, yada yada yada (aka, me).

I was exhausted and it wasn't even 8 am.

I had a litany of things to get done after dropping off said uniform to the school's front office and sending another text back to my college kid, trying to calm them down.

"It will be okay" I typed. "You are allowed to be human. Just explain what happened to the professor and try to let it go. Let me know how it goes. Love you."

Hmmm...

Perhaps I was trying to calm myself down at the same time.

As I pulled into my driveway, my jammie shirt peeking out from under the sweatshirt I had thrown on, I began to sob. I had tried to hide it and there it was, flailing about, showing the world that I do not have it together.

This mom gig is really hard.
And this mom of bigs gig feels harder than any other season.

Am I helping them too much?
Am I too tied up in my kids' success?
Am I still stuck on what will other people think?

Is that why I'm an absolute wreck right now?

I've read a thousand articles about how to never compare myself.
I've listened to podcasts about self-care and healthy boundaries.
I've laughed at social media videos about the reality of mom life.

But there I sat, trying to wipe back tears beginning to stain the sweatshirt that one of my bigs had given me for my birthday.

And then I laughed. Out loud.

Because there they were.

The words "JUST BREATHE" written beautifully (with a butterfly to boot - my favorite) across my chest.

I inhaled.

Long.
Slow.
Deep.

And while I held for the count of four (I've read that somewhere...I think it's called "box breathing"), I saw the basketball hoop at the end of the driveway and the half-pile of mulch that my other college kid (who was already home) had begun to spread in our landscaping.

I believe I exhaled at some point (I had to, right?).
But mostly I remembered that this is a FULL mom life.

Not an easy one. But a FULL one.

One where mornings are rough and we want to hide in our closets or cars.

But also one where we get to sit on the bleachers and watch our kids play their hearts out on the court, catching a glimpse of what makes their hearts come alive.

One where certain people forget certain things (like uniforms and waking up and not sending texts in ALL CAPS).

But also one where "I'm sorry"s are said and professors understand and we ALL have permission to be human.

Us and our kids.

We ALL have permission to do it right sometimes and wrong others.
To cry and to laugh with (and at) ourselves and each other.
To stay in our cars for as long as we need to and also cheer our hearts out on the sidelines. In the same day.

Isn't that what sharing this life together with our kids is all about?

Not having all our ducks in a row every single time.
Not remembering the uniforms and waking up on time and speaking in a gentle tone via text without ever skipping a beat.

Not being perfect. But being human.

And as long as we can remember that, I think we'll ALL be okay.

[Esther]

We all need moms who are
on the other side of whatever
season we're in.

Moms who can say,
"Hey, I was there too, and it was
hard and I didn't know how we were
going to make it to the other side,
but we did and you will too. You will
get to the other side. But for now,
you should know that you're
not alone. I'm here for you."

NEVER EMPTY NEST

6
STILL BECOMING

I didn't become your mom in a moment.

Not when the pregnancy test showed two lines.
Not when I labored for 15 hours.
Not when I held you for the first time.

I didn't become your mom in a span of nine months. Or in a moment's meeting.

I became your mom in the years before you were born, when I dreamt of being of mom.

I became your mom in the decades that followed. Decades filled to the brim with learning and unlearning and stumbling along and flying and with the both of us changing, changing, changing so much we'd be unrecognizable to our younger selves.

I became your mom every time I fought for you, held you, cried for you, felt my heart break when yours broke.

I became your mom when I stopped holding tightly to my dreams for you and began protecting the dreams you had for yourself.

I became your mom in the nights I didn't dream at all, but rather I laid awake, worrying about everything and nothing at all. Nights I waited for you to stop crying. Nights I waited for you to pull into the driveway.

Becoming your mom is just that.
Always that.
A becoming.

A constant becoming that doesn't end with fanfare and bullhorns at a certain age or on a specific day.

I am still becoming your mom. Figuring out how to love you best, in this moment in time.

Still trying to figure out this un-figure-outable motherhood thing.

I am not done becoming.

And neither, darling, are you.

[Melissa]

7
TWO SPOONS

I could see that she was holding back tears as she walked down the steps of the school bus and into the passenger seat of our family minivan.

The words came tumbling out like a waterfall, "He broke up with me at lunch."

My heart sank as I watched her body curl into a ball, her head flush against the window, tears flowing freely now.

"Oh honey. I'm so sorry. I know how much you liked him."

I laid my hand on her arm for a moment and she wrapped herself further into a ball. Silence ensued for the rest of our drive home.

She bolted into the house and to her room, shutting the door. I followed her up the stairs, and as I rested my head on her closed door, I could make out muffled sobs.

My heart sank even more. My girl was hurting. And no matter what I did or said in that moment, it probably wouldn't help at all. She was suffering the normal heartbreak that comes with first crushes, first kisses and first rejections.

I would just let her be for now, alone with her own heart and all the feelings that were new and confusing and downright difficult. It was the best and only thing I knew to do. It seemed to be what she wanted and needed the most.

I meandered to the kitchen, not sure what to do with myself. I wanted to run right back upstairs and wipe her tears away with a kiss, a hug, an emotional bandaid, an "I love you" or one of the other many mom tricks I had up my sleeve.

Not this time.

Instead, all I could do was pray (and I sure did) and feel awkward and start to make dinner.

Time seemed to march ever so slowly that afternoon, as it does when pain is loud for us or someone we love. Time feels achingly long and almost cruel. Why can't it pass quickly so that we are on the other side of loss and grief and back to our hopeful selves?

How I wished that for her that insufferable day.

Right before dinner, there was a knock at our front door. Odd at that time of day.

I glanced through the window and right in front of my own teary eyes, one of my daughter's best friends was anxiously standing there, carrying two spoons and a huge container of my girl's favorite ice cream flavor.

I opened the door, gave her a quick, thankful hug and whispered, "She's up in her room."

I heard another knock, footsteps, a door open and then shut again.

What a strange and hard afternoon for my mama self. Yet somehow wonderful and what I hoped for all at the same time.

What I couldn't do anymore as a mom (as much as I desperately wanted to), her friend was able to do. Listen. Relate. Comfort. Eat ice cream out of the container right before dinner.

All so normal for that season of her life.

I kept milling around the kitchen, gratitude welling up inside of me for this friendship that my daughter had.

The kind that goes to the grocery store instead of her dance practice.
The kind that shows up instead of stays away.
The kind that hangs out with the tears and not only the laughs.

I heard the front door close and a car pull away.

In what seemed like only a few moments, her friend was gone again, just like that.

Had it been enough for that very miserable afternoon?

I wondered what would happen next.

Only moments went by when I heard the familiar creaking of my girl's door opening and loud footsteps down the stairs.

She bounded into the kitchen, hair a mess, eyes all puffy, but the next words out of her mouth were priceless.

"I'm going to be okay, Mom, even if I'm not right now."

She threw her arms around me and we hugged for a long time and as I held her close, I knew deep inside that it had all been enough.

"What's for dinner?" she quietly asked.

As we unwrapped ourselves, I whispered one last thing into her ear, "I made your favorite."

[Esther]

8
NOT READY

I'm not ready.

To start packing up his room--his clothes and his computer and his life here--and resume another life as an RA, as a junior in college (what?!?), as an kid/adult that may or may not come back to live at home next summer.

I'm not ready for less conversations with him. Right now I can catch him after work or before he goes to the movies with a friend or on the weekend when he's just waking up, and we can chat about anything, everything.

Soon he will be busy with dorm life and media classes and poker nights and e-sports practice.

Soon life will take him away again.

The one constant...

Change.

The ebb and flow of gripping tightly and letting go reluctantly. The friction of grief and joy.

I'm not ready.

To go school shopping for her, which is maybe her favorite part of school, and watch her go through her closet to see what items she is lacking, and prepare for her to begin her senior year of high school.

She is the baby, and I'm not ready for all the lasts with her. I weep just thinking about it.

I will watch her and her friends pile in the car with their water bottles and blankets to head to their last homecoming.

I will be in the crowd, witnessing the last race of her high school career.

I will buy the dress and tell her she looks ridiculously beautiful and pose with her for pictures before her senior prom.

I will stop myself there, hard stop, because I cannot think about graduation.

This is what we prepare 18 years for, but I can tell you right now that even another decade wouldn't be enough.

I must loosen my grip, cheer them on as they become, as they are becoming, and leave a healthy dose of room for the relationship to morph fully into something else: friendship.

I pray the connections we've created, with the tears and laughter of their childhoods, the showing up in all the ways, the hugs and the "you are amazing"s and the "I love you"s will hold.

I hope my grieving doesn't overshadow the immense pride I feel every time I see their faces.

I have spent two decades pouring into them. That won't stop.

Momming doesn't ever.

Today I will sit in my not readiness and be okay in it.

[Melissa]

9
ON LEAVING THE NEST

The happy and dreaded time arrives.

One of my bigs is ready to leave the nest.

The soft one.
The stable one.
The safe one.

The one I've tried so hard to make this way.

With twigs of understanding.
With leaves of love.
With branches of respect.

Even some mud of toughness.
Some odds-and-ends of independence.
And also some of my own mom saliva of sass and strength.
(look it up. birds do this weird thing.)

It's not a perfect nest.
It's messy.
And full of bits and pieces of this and that.

But it's mine. And it's his.

At dinner, I plug along, carefree and happy, all right with my world, then there it is.

THE QUESTION.

"Mom, will you help me with my resume?"

My heart does its all-too-familiar mom dance.

It's proud. It's happy. It's sad. It's overwhelmed. It doesn't quite know what it is.

"Of course," I reply, cool as a cucumber, but simmering underneath like soup in a pot on a crisp fall day.

We sit side-by-side, in his post-college room, screens glaring in front of us, resume front and center.

We chat.
We fix.
We laugh.

I cry (just a little) hopefully without him seeing.

We talk about all the far-away jobs he's applying to.
We act like it's just another DAY in the life.

And it is.
But it also isn't.

Because no one ever told me that my heart would pound out of my chest with unconditional love the DAY I brought this snuggly (and kind of ugly) baby home from the hospital.

And no one ever shared with me that I would not know what to do with myself the DAY he got on the big yellow school bus for kindergarten.

And I had zero idea that I would silently hold back tears on the DAY we stood back-to-back and for the first time, and he was taller than me.

And now, what is this? My boy. I can hardly get my thoughts on paper. On this DAY, my boy is ready to fly.

Out into the hard.
The unknown.
The scary.

He should.

He'll leave behind the soft.
The stable.
The safe.

He should.

I'll worry (don't all moms all the time about everything anyway?).
I'll cry.
I'll cheer.

I'll text him too much.
I'll check in on him too much.
I'll do all the mom things that I'm not supposed to do anymore too much.

But I will never, ever, ever, ever love this boy too much.

[Esther]

10
GOOD MOM

I am a good mom.

I had no idea what I was doing when I started. Who does? I had ideas and dreams and plans, but when does anything in life go accordingly?

I was young. Not crazy young, but young enough feel like a baby myself. Becoming a mom at the tender age of 22 was a surprise and so utterly terrifying, but I had loved kids since I WAS one myself and I knew I was born for it.

I was unmarried. To say that it didn't fit THE PLAN of my conservative upbringing would be accurate and kind of an understatement.

I had to go to my pastor and apologize. Mmmm-hmmmm.

But I wasn't sorry.

I was a good mom. I worried like mad and feared I was going to mess my kids up for life and kept track of every little detail of their lives and doted on them.

I let my three-year old son sleep on a little pullout couch in our bedroom for a year because he had night terrors and wanted to be near me.

I carried my daughter on my hip until she was four. Because I could not resist her slender arms and the need in her eyes and when she reached up for me, reaching back for her was just instinctual.

I was a good mom.

I took my son to the doctor when his mental health was so bad that he was scaring all of us. He was isolating and making morbid comments and his shine had gone away so gradually, we didn't notice at first.

I sat in the doctor's office and could not slow my heart rate, but I applied calm to my face like a moisturizer and rubbed his shoulder in support.

I picked up my daughter from school 30 miles away during Covid when she was still doing in-person classes because her anxiety was paralyzing her and she couldn't stand to be there one more minute. Even though she had just gotten off the morning bus.

I let them have mental health days where they didn't go anywhere, not to school or practice, but got to sleep in and just have a day to recalibrate.

I am a good mom.

I am affectionate and patient and I listen. I get snappy and distracted and over-tired. I show up. I over-extend. I love hard and hold on too tight.

I still worry. I still fear I am messing them up. But I know I am doing my best.

I am a good mom.

At the end of the day and the end of my life, that is one thing I am sure of.

[Melissa]

What moms text:

"Having fun?"

**What moms hope they
get the answer to:**

**Who are you with?
When will you be home?
Are you in any kind of trouble?
Are you alive?**

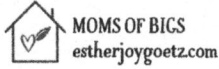

11
I'D RATHER

I'd rather my children be critical thinkers than go along with any crowd.

That includes...

school
our family
church
their friends
a particular political group
their partner
or even the latest blow up on the internet.

I'd rather they...

question
doubt
debate
discover
expand
rediscover
imagine
and create

than lose the unique person they were created to be.

I don't want them to agree when they don't

or

stand against something just to fit in.

I'd rather have them wrestle with the nuances and the grays of life than be consumed with the black and white.

It will be harder for them, but so much better.
It will be harder for the people around them, but also so much better.

I'd rather have them...

be kind than be right
be wise than follow the rules
be courageous than be liked

It's not an easy path.

It's...

Twisty-turny.
Bumpy.
Confusing.
Daring.
Filled with obstacles.

But it's a beautiful path.

Hopeful.
Truthful.
Enlightening.
Adventurous.
Filled with wonder.

I'd rather my kids...

follow their big dreams and their big hearts than conform to boxes built to keep them small.

love with abandon than live someone else's dream.

uncover who they really are way down inside than stay hidden from themselves and the world.

It's one of the greatest gifts I can give to my kids...

The permission to be completely themselves.

[Esther]

12
MARTYRS

Moms, we were never meant to be martyrs.

We are not supposed to do it all and lose ourselves in the process.

We were never meant to be so giving that we gave all of ourselves away--piece by piece, year by year.

We don't need to be Superwoman.

And we certainly don't need to be anybody else besides ourselves.

We don't need to be everything and we can't.
It's all an illusion anyway.

The perfect family, the clean house, the flawless marriage, the well-behaved kids... It's all bull****.

We do not have to have it all figured out. We don't need to pretend like we know what we're doing.

Our kids mess up. They get into trouble or fail a class or hang out with the wrong kids or don't take our well-meaning advice.

They are on their phones 24/7 or they leave messes everywhere or they don't make curfew or they make us cry in the middle of the night.

And we lose our temper or get fast food several times a week or forget to sign all the permission slips or we fantasize about running away for a weekend or a month.

This is motherhood.

It's painful and messy and joyous and triumphant.
It's shame and pride and do overs and I love yous.
It's exhaustion and elation.

We don't have to do everything, be everyone, take care of it all.

We are not martyrs.

We are women.
We are moms.
We are wounded and whole and flawed and holy.

The best, most indestructible quality we have is our love.
And we definitely have that in spades.

[Melissa]

13
SAFE

I couldn't get it out of my mind.

Am I a safe mom?

With all that's going on in the world right now, this phrase kept running through my brain.
And it got louder and louder.

Would my kids be able to tell me anything?

Without fear?

Of judgment?
Shame?
Or agendas?

Would they be able to tell me what's eating them up inside?

Would they be able to come to me if they had a huge, scary decision that seems to have "no exact right answer?"

Would they feel like I'm the very first person they would want to tell?

It's easy to be a "safe" place when our kids come to us with their successes.

"I got an A."
"I scored a goal."
"I left that party because everyone was drinking."

And we respond with "woohoo" and a hug and a "good for you."

But what about their struggles?
What about the really hard parts of their lives?

The parts that might freak us out?
Or make us wonder if we've done or are doing a bad job?
The parts that will tap into our fear or shame?

Being the "get it out in the open mom," I mustered up my gumption to ask one of them, the one who probably would know the answer because they've felt unsafe in the past and have let me know the truth in no uncertain terms.

And also because she's had a front-row seat to the way I've tried so hard to grow and learn.

As moms, one of our most important jobs is to be a safe space.

To make our "nests" a soft place to land when their world is hard.

To listen and respond without some kind of mom agenda (something the bid kid I asked highlighted in her answer back to me after she said, "sometimes yes and other times, not really").

To wrap our arms and hearts around them while navigating all our own feelings later with our safe people.

This is no easy task.
It might be the hardest mom assignment of all.

I know it is for me.

But I'm determined to keep growing and learning and changing and dealing with my own unsafe stuff inside so that my kids can come to me with...

anything

AND

everything.

No matter what they've done. Think. Has happened to them. Or might do.

I want them be completely confident that all they will get from me in return is open arms enveloping them with real-without-conditions love.

[Esther]

14
THE THING

Encourage your kid to find their thing.

The Thing.

The Thing that they can't stop thinking about doing, lights them up like a wildfire leveling everything in its path.

It doesn't matter what that Thing is. If you get it or not. Even if you are convinced it will ruin them and you lie awake at night wondering in which specific way it might ruin them.

Do everything in your power to support them doing their Thing. Even if it takes monumental sacrifice.

Show up at every performance or race or contest or recital or tournament of the Thing.

Cheer them on loudy and perhaps even commission a giant cardboard cutout of their face to hold up while they do their Thing.

It's great if they are next-level at it but that's just the icing. Their joy is the whole dang cake.

Because this Thing that they love doing, that they practice and hone and dedicate their whole self to, gives them so much back.

Self-confidence. Dedication. Perseverance. Self-love. Joy.

It gives them Their Voice.

It gives them Their People. The ones who love it as much as they do, that they can talk for hours about all the details of it that no one else understands.

Be a constant cheerleader of the Thing.

Get up early and drive an obscene amount of miles and pay ridiculous money to love what they love.

Their heart doesn't deceive them. It is their lighthouse, guiding them to the safety of their own inherent self.

They know what they want.

And oh, how your eyes will fill every time you get to watch them

DO the Thing and

Shine.

[Melissa]

15
NOT.A.DARN.THING.

I was driving up the hill that leads to our home thinking about my four kids, and I just started to cry.

Because you know...

Each one of them is struggling...

With something.

Something that I can probably blame on myself.

My lack of whatever. My too much of whatever.

What I modeled. What they absorbed from said modeling.

Too much helping.
Not enough just "being."
People-pleasing.
Savior complexes.
Workaholism.

The "apple-doesn't-fall-far-from-the-tree" somethings.

As I dug a little deeper, it struck me that some of what they are struggling with has NOTHING to do with me.

NOT.A.DARN.THING.

It comes from the fact that they are humans in a human world filled with all the human things.

No one is not struggling.
No one's life travels only up and to the right.
No one doesn't feel the weight of the hard and the heavy.

And my precious kids are part of that fragile humanity, one that is scary and gorgeous and awful and holy and every last thing in between.

I thought when I had clarity in that moment that it wasn't ALL.MY.FAULT, the tears would dry up and I would pull into my driveway a little lighter.

Instead, they flowed more freely and I had to stop and pull over.

Because this whole bringing into and trying to raise and watching our kids navigate this beautiful mess of the world that we ALL live in isn't for the faint of heart.

It's such a huge risk.
It needs so much bravery.
It requires being able to sit in the struggle and cry tears on your way up your hill in your car.

As I sat on the side of the curb in stunned silence, the salty drops navigating their way down to my chin before I wiped them away, I couldn't help but think how so much of motherhood is done in the spaces where no one else is.

Where it's just us. All by ourselves.

Sometimes crying.
Oftentimes praying.
All the time loving.

Not in the way we imagined at the start of it all.
But in ALL.THE.WAYS. that matter in the end.

[Esther]

My Son,

The world might see you as a man, but I will always see you as the boy who completely captured my heart.

NEVER EMPTY NEST

16
THE BATHROOM STALL

I used to cry in a bathroom stall every morning before the bell rang.

14 was my roughest age by far.

Too shy, too quiet, too skinny, glasses way too big.

Too little of all the things that I thought might make me a better version of myself.

More confident or popular or even just good ENOUGH to get through the day without stifling sobs in a bathroom stall.

My own skin made me itchy.

I wanted to be anyone else but me.

Years later, my 14-year daughter called me from school to pick her up because she had a panic attack so bad she threw up in a bathroom stall.

She felt alone and judged and different and depressed.
And she wanted to be anyone else but her.

The 14-year old girl in me wanted to scream and cry and say "You too?"

Hearing the pain in her voice unraveled me. It made me re-live my own unprocessed pain from a period in time when I did not want to exist on this planet.

It destroyed me to witness that in her, too.

I had to grieve for me and my girl.

So I picked her up and held her and let her take mental health days when she needed them and we talked and cried and took it one day at a time.

I survived 14.
She survived 14.

Not everyone does.

So we need to keep talking about mental health and giving our kids the space to talk about their dark thoughts and their sadness and LISTEN, really LISTEN, to what they are going through.

Our kids need to be heard.
My daughter needed to be heard.
14-year old me needed to be heard.

I'm listening.

[Melissa]

17
WILD HORSES

"Are we going to see the wild horses?" my not-yet-college-bound, have-to-be-dragged-everywhere, youngest asked. "You promised."

We were on a college visit trip with her older brother. Five colleges in five days.

The drive to see these mythical creatures on an exotic island was about an hour out of the way and I was exhausted from tours about professors/safety/dorms and hotel rooms with weird smells/bad breakfasts/non-working hot tubs.

But my memory of the picture on the cover of the book, *Misty of Chincoteague*, a beautiful wild horse and her foal, drew me in and convinced me to keep my promise.

As we pulled in to the park and made our way to the restrooms before embarking on our glorious, out-of-the-way adventure, signs warned not to feed the horses as they may bite and to ensure our safety by staying 40-feet away. This was exciting!

Bladders empty, we were ready! We couldn't wait to see these wild creatures, prancing in the sand dunes and uttering high-pitched neighs.

What happened next was stranger than strange.

We rounded the corner and there was a horse, in the middle of the parking lot. Not prancing. Not neighing. Standing. Still. So still, we thought it might be a taxidermist's latest "stuffed" project.

We got out. Walked around it. It did NOT move. Just stood there. We did see it take a breath, so we surmised it was alive and didn't belong at the local Cabela's.

We had so hoped to happen upon a wild, prancing, neighing horse, enjoying the sands of Virginia beaches and its ability to roam FREE.

But what we found was more like a TAMED mule ready to plow the fields under the guise of some master who needed to get things done.

As we ventured on the park pathways, we saw a few more horse-mules milling around, and I can assure you that we were not scared, or excited, not even one little bit.

We got back in our cars and my mom thoughts took off into those mom places only they can go.

Are these horses like my kids?

Longing for adventure, FREEDOM, and curiosity to discover, hope and dream?

But standing around, TAMED, bored and controlled because of how me, as a mom, and society, as a whole, has directed them?

Don't bite.
Stand still.
Be quiet.

Don't stand up for yourself (your true self). Fit in.
Do what everyone else is doing. Stay in the box.
Control yourself at all costs. Never color outside of the lines.

College visits.
What everyone else did.
What we were supposed to do.

Over the next days, I kept coming back and back to my thoughts about these horse-mules and my kids.

I did not want them to be mules. I wanted them to be horses. WILD ONES. Not TAMED into submission by some arbitrary set of rules that who-knows-who made up.

I wanted them to be FREE. To discover, hope and dream.

I talked and talked and talked to them about it. And then talked some more.

Guess what happened?

My college-bound son said, "NOPE."
He decided to take a gap year.
He enjoyed his senior year without the pressure of choosing.
He never went to any of those five colleges visited on that trip.
He discovered a school that made his heart happy a whole year later.

FREEDOM.

My baby watched him intently.
She spent an extra year with him, becoming the best of friends. When it was her turn, she chose an out-of-the-box school and got her Bachelor's degree in two years. Two long, hard years. She moved to California at 19 to pursue her dreams, graduation behind her.
She wants to win an Emmy.

FREEDOM.

Guess what else happened?

I began to wonder the same thing about me.

Do I have the FREEDOM to discover, hope and dream?

As a middle-aged, regular, mom who has always played by the rules?
Who didn't bite, stood still and was quiet?

The answer: YES. YES I DO.

I might stand up for myself.
What if I forge my own way?
Maybe I will even draw my own lines to color inside.
We'll see how it all plays out.
It's going to be good.

FREEDOM.

[Esther]

18
A THOUSAND SUNRISES

Your strength, dear daughter, scares them.
Your opinions are too much for them.

They don't understand your eclectic style.
They wish you had a filter on that mouth.

They try to shut you up, but a finger over your lips cannot silence your ideals. They want to contain your flames so that you don't burn the town down with them in it.

You are too bright for them; so bright it makes their eyes water when they stare too long.

The fight in you exhausts them, a pitbull whose jaw will not slacken.

They try to pour salt in your wounds.
You don't hide your scars.

You pull back the curtain and put a spotlight on them.

They are accessories. A feather boa billowing around your shoulders. Yellow streamers in your hair.

Let them be scared, dear daughter.
Let them try to figure you out.
Let them try to tape you up in a box, label you, and ship you to off to a far-away land.

It cannot be done.

You are a thousand sunrises behind closed eyelids--lights exploding and colors undulating like Caribbean waves.

You are thunder at midnight, cracking the walls, eroding foundations.

You are a backyard full of fireflies on a muggy August night.

You are an arrow--sharp and precise--shot in a perfect delicate arc.

Blowing kisses as you sail overhead.

[Melissa]

19
TEARS

Mom tears are a thing.

A downright, real, can't-get-around-it thing.

They start as soon as we see our newborn, all bloody and beautiful.

Show up when our kindergartener waves through the bus window.

Flow at graduations and midnight prayers and drop offs at college campuses.

At times, they are cheery, accompanied by smiles full of hope and joy and pride.

Other times, they flow uncontrollably in the shower, our broken hearts pleading with God to help us help them.

They often just show up. Unannounced. It doesn't take much.

It could be the simple mom twinge that reminds us that it's all going to change much too soon.

Mom tears are a thing.

My far-away daughter texted me a picture of our latest weekend together.

It had been a time of laughter and lollipops and late nights.

A time for talks and hugs and dog walks.
A time to watch sports and play outside and paddle kayaks.
A time for junk food and angel food cake and "Happy Birthday."

A wonderful, happy, beautiful time.

Tears bubbled without warning and I wiped them away quickly.

But then I just stood there.
And let them come.
Not trying to stop them.

They trickled out slowly and were gone before I knew it.

I was so very glad for them.

They reminded me I am loved and grateful and sad.
That life is gorgeous and hard and sacred.

But most of all, they gave honor to my full-to-the-brim-and-overflowing mom heart, sometimes leaking out as salty drops down my cheeks.

Mom tears are a thing.
A very good thing.

{Esther]

20
A PILE OF JOY

Who knew a pile of joy would be a bunch of giant shoes in a big heap right inside the door?

Each pair of shoes representing a person's feet who I hope always feels welcome walking through my door.

No matter the day or time.

I hope the ringing laughter that accompanies the kicking off of these shoes gets infused into the walls and floorboards and spreads into the roof shingles and foundation.

I hope everyone in these rooms feels loved and accepted.

Most of these shoes belong to kids who met years ago and have stayed friends.

Who have helped each other navigate parents' illnesses, their own depression, bad grades, and Covid isolation; who have celebrated each other's birthdays and graduations and had countless pizza parties and sleepovers.

They have endured disappointments and celebrated each other's successes. These shoes and personalities have grown and worn into themselves.

But they are, at their core, still kids.

Longing to have a kite of freedom billowing in the wind, while delicately tethered to the home of their childhood.

A home that wraps them in warmth and comfort.
A home where they can unencumberedly BE themselves.
A home that always has a light on for them.

There will always be space for shoe piles by the door.

And the higher it gets, the happier I am.

[Melissa]

Being a mom of big kids means worrying, praying, worrying some more, praying even more and repeating this for the rest of your life.

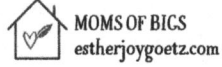

MOMS OF BIGS
estherjoygoetz.com

21
THE VOW

It all started a whole bunch of long times ago in the vow I made to myself.

[MY KIDS WOULD BE WELL-BEHAVED]

And by well-behaved, I meant sitting still with a smile on their face in church and school, obeying my every command the first time, keeping their rooms clean (and the bathroom too) and getting high marks at school and always always always doing their best no matter what they were doing...on the field, their chores, practicing their instrument.

There would be none of this nonsense like talking back to me, rolling their eyes behind their teachers' backs, getting speeding tickets, sneaking around, and God-forbid, never any drugs or alcohol or sex or smoking or any of those super scary and awful things that could have life-long, damaging effects...or so I was told and believed.

But then, of course, my vow was tested at every turn.

Littles throwing temper tantrums in grocery stores.
Middles lighting fires in our garage with Bic lighters and gasoline in water guns.
And bigs doing many of those "God-forbid" things.

I was raising actual people who had never made that vow and didn't care if it was broken every which way.

They were curious and testing boundaries and trying on "hats" to see which ones fit and figuring out their own paths the way I had and my parents had (and all the generations that camebefore them), with all the foibles and triumphs and struggles and successes that come from being an actual, real live human being.

At first, I fought it with all my might.
I vowed to keep the vow I made.

So I clamped down, trying to control every mood and behavior, especially the God-forbid ones.

But as you can guess, my kids still kept being actual people (imagine that).

And $*@T kept hitting the fan.

Over and over again.

One had debilitating anxiety and OCD.
Another had off-the-charts ADHD.
Still another flew under the radar, all the while doing whatever the heck he wanted to do while visibly complying.
And lastly, one became an expert at sneaking around.

And that vow I kept trying to keep?

It shattered right in front of my very own mom eyes. And heart.

I thought I was a bad mom. That my kids were hopeless.

Until...
Until...

I found out a little secret about parenting and parenthood and kids and moms and all of us people, old and young, ADHD and OCD, sneaky and outwardly compliant.

It was never my job to make sure my kids were perfectly well-behaved (or even me for that matter).

It is always my job to help them figure out who they really are and what they actually love.

To be themselves in a world that tells them to be everything but and to find out what makes their hearts sing, come alive and dance a little jig.

And that little secret helped me to breathe a big, long, deep mom sigh of relief.

No more unnecessary and impossible vow that choked the life out of all of us.

Yes, my kids still had ADHD and OCD.
They were still sneaky and outwardly compliant.
My heart still raced every time they did those God-forbid things [oh, and it still does].

But I got to see all the beauty of their humanity and their individuality and STILL DO.

The creative genius and fierce tenderness of one.
The ability to truly connect with everyone and anyone at anytime of another.
The undying curiosity and steady loyalty of yet another.
And the beautiful empathy, fiery independence of still another.

Here I am, laying in my bed, typing on my keyboard and I know that you have so many things on your mom plate right now.

So many kids who might be in the middle of the struggle of their lives.

So much heartache and God-forbid things happening day after day.

It's a lot.
It's hard.

So I'm here to remind you that there is great hope.

You will make it until tonight and then tomorrow and then the next day.
And we are ALL allowed to be human, whatever that means, with all our very own fits and starts and scary and joy.

Us.
And our kids.

Here's to tossing all our vows out the window and watching them break into a million pieces.

Here's to the freedom to be ourselves.

[Esther]

22
UNTIL HE WASN'T

Once upon a time, my kid stopped talking.

He hit the teens years so hard, he clammed up.

As a little boy he talked my ever-loving ear off. He had more questions than I could answer. He was a million-watt bulb that every creature and human wanted to be near.

He was pure sunshine.
Until he wasn't.

As a teen, he struggled with mental health and isolated. He shut down and stopped talking. And storms rolled in under his skin.

I was powerless to stop it, like every mom who desperately wants to fix life's unfixable things and take her kid's pain away.

But I held on.

I missed my little boy with a force that took my breath right out of my lungs. I grieved.

I kept engaging with him, even when I would get one word answers.

I leaned in his doorway just so I could be near him. Even if we said nothing. I left his favorite snack on his desk while he was gaming.

I reminded him that I was there, always, if he needed anything.

Then one day my not-so-sunshiney boy graduated and went off to college and a light switch flipped back on.

The clouds over his head rolled out and the sky in his eyes cleared.

He opened up to the world again.

And now this kid of mine, not so much a kid anymore, loves filling me in on all.the.things and asking my advice and making me laugh.

We have long conversations late into the night and when he needs me, however and whenever that is,

I am always right here.

[Melissa]

23
PAPER CHAINS

Once upon a time, a mom of an 18-year-old made a paper chain.

Just like the ones her kids made in preschool, but this one tucked neatly in her head.

She almost made a real one, but thought it would cause a ruckus in her home.

Why? Why?
Why the paper chain?

Because she was counting down the days until her son left for college.

It all started in the middle of the winter.
This mental paper chain.
180 days.

It wasn't because he was a horrible, disrespectful teen

OR

that she was a terrible mom, even though she felt like it often (she had a paper chain after all).

It wasn't because he was breaking curfew every day and doing all kinds of god-knows-what

OR

maybe she was just clueless...which was more likely.

It wasn't because she didn't love him, because moms just can't help themselves and she loved this kid especially

OR

that he didn't have friends or wasn't enjoying high school.

It wasn't because he bought a Mustang convertible and got in an accident with his younger brother in the back seat during the aftermath of a hurricane

OR

that she had told him not to go out more than a couple of times.

Why then?

Why? Why?
Why the paper chain?

It was because he was fighting to be himself, a grown-up

AND

she was confused about that and didn't quite know what to do. And she was tired of the fighting.

It was because he wanted to be with his friends more than he wanted to be home for dinner

AND

that made her pretty sad and sometimes, even angry.

It was because he wanted to explore new scary out-of-the-box adventures

AND

she was freaking out inside and maybe it would be easier for her if he was out of her sight, not so much in her face.

It was (REALLY) in the end, because he was spreading his wings to fly on his own

AND

she knew he would soar (or maybe fall to the ground, get back up again and then stumble along until he took flight).

It wasn't very long until those 180 "circles" of paper were ripped completely off, with none remaining.

They were scattered all over the floor of her memories.

He left.
She cried.
She cried some more.

She went home and made another paper chain.
This one counting the days until he came back home.

[Esther]

24
I KNOW YOU

I can never un-see the baby boy who, the first time I laid eyes on him, made me weep.

He looked at me with translucent eyes.
Eyes that said, "I know you."

He wailed the entire first night in the hospital and I wept more. I was 22 years old and I had no idea what I was doing. I was the kind of exhausted that no amount of sleep could touch.

The magnitude of just keeping him alive, much less flourishing, sent me into a ferocious post-partum panic attack.

That whole first night felt like a lifetime.

Once home we fell into an easy rhythm that he led. He was my teacher. He grew to be a laidback baby with an infectious giggle and the most perfect, heart-melting smile.

And those eyes. They held truth and oceans and sea glass and star dust. They were entire universes.

I look at him now, 20 years old, not too far off from how old I was when I had him.

He is this now-version of him but he is also that then-version baby and if I had known how much I would love him it might've been unbearable.

I feel the weight of loving a child so much it hurts in the best, most exquisite way possible.

I hold them both now.

Him and my memories of him, in tandem, my cup full, love spilling over the edges.

[Melissa]

25
FLY

Like what I like.
Think how I think.
Do what I do.
Be who I am.

For years, this was my life's mantra, and thus my mom mantra.

Make decisions quickly.
Enjoy watching football.
Be an extrovert.
Believe every doctrine I espouse about God.

On and on the list went, my secret goal to transform my kids into my spitting image.

It was not ill-intentioned. I thought I was doing life right.
But it wasn't good, healthy or loving.

I was missing out on the beauty of diversity among my kids. They were all so different and I had much to learn from each one of them.

I was missing out on how my kids would challenge me, show me something new that I had never experienced before and perhaps would really enjoy, and speak into the parts of me that needed to change.

I was missing out on my actual kids. What they like and don't. What brings them joy. What causes them pain and disgust and perhaps makes them angry. Who they ARE underneath all the outer pretenses and baggy clothes.

Gradually, the "scales" fell off my eyes and I could see this crucial life lesson: these people are NOT me, NOR should they be.

And my mom job was to help them figure that out and cheer them on.

It's our child's job to try on all the different hats of life to see which might feel good, fit well, and they want more of.

Some of them might be the hats we wear and others would not feel good on our own heads.

It's part of the process for them to become adults and more importantly, themselves.

It's not easy. We are stretched farther than we ever thought possible as we put aside our likes and our longings and choose to release them into the adventure of their own journeys!

But it IS where life becomes fuller than I thought possible.

Where I have "tried on" some of their hats and found them to fit just right.

Where my love's root can dig deep and blossom into a big diverse bouquet.

It means allowing each of my kids to be perfectly themselves without an agenda in my back pocket.

It means receiving the variety of gifts that each one brings, gifts I would never receive if they were just like me.

It's not about having a bunch of "mini-mes" jumbled together at the holidays or on the latest family vacation, but about having a whole group of "yous" that come together to form a beautiful, colorful, and mixed up "us."

And as we say in our house, "trail mix is a lot more fun than eating a whole bag of peanuts."

So here's my final thought for my kids...

Like what YOU like.
Think how YOU think.
Do what YOU do.
Be who YOU are.

These are YOUR wings of freedom to be completely yourself.

Fly.
Fly.
Fly.

[Esther]

Say yes to the late-night convos.
The Taco Bell runs. The last-minute
shopping trips. The ordering pizza.
The helping with homework.
Say yes to the messes.
The chauffering.
The inconveniences.
The piles of shoes by the door
and mountains of laundry
by the washer.
There is a big-kid-sized hole left
when those things are gone.

26
AN OPEN LETTER

An open letter to younger me (with a then 13-year old daughter),

Take the hugs.
Take the selfies.
Take the "I love you"s.
Every last one.

Soon, mama, you will be "Bruh" to her.

The placing-her-hand-on-yours to-measure-how-big-her hands-are-compared-to-yours will be a thing of the past.

The cute poses and teeth-baring grins for pictures will be old news.

She will deem every picture you take of her disgusting.

She will run from hugs.

She will want to be behind closed doors more than in open spaces.

Her voice will deepen a little along with her hurts.
Her sarcasm will grow. Exponentially.

Hold 13-year-old her as long as she will let you.

14, 15-year-old her will change you as a mother in ways you won't see coming.
It will trigger your own past teen traumas.

You will see teen you in her and it will nearly break you.

And you will also rejoice in her. She will become stronger. Wiser. In such a short time.

She will teach you things.

You will grow right alongside her.

For now, watch her do flips into the ball pit at gymnastics. Dance with her in the kitchen. Blast Taylor Swift. Fill her water bottle before ski practice. Pull her hair back from her face as she throws up. Blow her kisses goodnight.

For now, capture her sparkle.
Hold her slender fingers in yours.
Cherish that beautiful, captivating girl.

Because you will blink...

...and she will be a woman.

[Melissa]

27
Y-E-S

When your big kid texts, "Can I come home for the weekend?" you jump at the chance and say a resounding "Y-E-S."

When your big kid pulls in the driveway, you run outside, wave frantically and give her a hug like you haven't seen her in five years (even though it's only been five weeks).

When your big kid dumps her stuff all over your kitchen counter, you hold your tongue and remember that it's only for a couple of days, knowing secretly you miss the "mess."

When your big kid asks, "Mom, do you have _____," you search your house until _____ is found underneath the sink in the back corner.

When your big kid rakes the leaves into a pile on your driveway, plops herself right in the middle, throwing them into the air because fall is her favorite season ever, you take a video and post it everywhere.

When your big kid holds her dad's hand during your lazy, long leaf-peeping walk, you watch from behind and your heart almost bursts because you love her more today than you ever have. And you had no idea this was possible.

When your big kid snuggles with you on the couch, watching football and eating popcorn, the official family snack, memories flood your mind of a little girl spinning in a circle humming while she eats the fluffy white goodness. A lump forms in your throat.

When your big kid gets ready to leave, you help pack her car, make sure she has air in that tire with the flashing light on, make a bag of goodies for her two-hour ride, and give her another hug like you won't see her again for another five years (even though it will only be five weeks).

When your big kid pulls out of your driveway, you shout "I love you," hands flailing in the air, as tears well in your eyes and you allow them to flow. Your heart is sad and thankful all at the same time.

When your big kid texts you, "Here," you breathe a long, mom sigh of relief, anticipating the next time you will be given another chance to jump and say a resounding "Y-E-S!"

[Esther]

28
CLOSED DOOR

Sometimes love is standing outside a closed door.

My beloved teen, I do that sometimes.

When you're angry or upset or hormonal or sad.
And you shut everyone out as you shut your door.

I know better than to press.
Your threshold has caution tape around it.

[Literally]

I remember being your age and shutting out the world.

Parents, friends, hope, joy.
All of it at once.
Swiftly. Resolutely.

Door and heart. SHUT.

I wonder if my mom cried on the other side of my door, like I do now.

I want to fix it. I want to scoop my bigger-than-me you into my arms.

I want to wipe your eyes like I did when you were little. A quick sweep of the hand, snuggly kisses, "I love you"s. Your fat, swollen tears dissolved in my palms.

You feel alone in there, I am sure of it.
Abandoned. Discontent. Burning in your veins.

Feeling like no one has ever felt what you are feeling. How could they possibly?

My hand is on the doorknob, waiting for you to call me in.
You don't.

You need all that space for your pain to exist in.
You want to sit in it.

You want to give it a name, with flourishes and underlines, but you can't. It won't be summarized with some ink on a crumpled up piece of paper.

You want it to frantically lap at your chin as you struggle to breathe.

You need to feel desperate.
It helps you feel alive instead of numb.

I know.

I listen. I don't hear anything.

My hand slips off the knob and I walk down the hall, away from you.

Rooms away. Worlds away.

I sit in my own pain. The pain of that door between us.
It isn't your moods that trouble me. I get it.

It's the closed door that is hardest to endure.

[Melissa]

29
LITTLE BROWN BAG

What is in the little brown bag I have sitting on the car seat next to me?

If I showed you, it probably wouldn't mean anything to you.

In fact, you might be like, "Who cares? So what? I don't get it."

But if I told you (and I just might) why it says "(heart), Mom," it probably would mean a lot to you.

In fact, you might be like, "Aha! Yup. I get it now."

That's because it's a mom thing inside the brown bag.

A mom thing in the form of a Taylor Ham (yes, I'm from North Jersey and that's what we call it here) and egg (no cheese, no ketchup) on an "everything" bagel from our local bagel shop.

And not just from any local bagel shop.

The one we drive all.the.way to (now that we moved 30 minutes away) just to get this one-of-a-kind deliciousness.

The one where memories have formed with friends and family and foe alike.

The very particular (as in the only) one my son not-so-secretly loves and would eat every day.

This mom thing happens to every single mom (I'm pretty sure).

We are "out and about" doing mom stuff or not mom stuff (it doesn't matter) and our kid pops right into our brain.

Thoughts jump around.

"I'm totally going to stop and get the treat they love so much."
"But it's pretty far out of the way."
"Who cares?"

Somehow, someway, no matter what kind of tasks we are doing or how much extra time it will take, we rearrange our lives all so we can stop in THAT place to get them their favorite.

Walking back out to our car, treat in hand, our hearts have a little jolt of mom joy.

We can't wait to see the look on their face as we place it in their ever-loving hands.
We might even get a hug and a "thanks, Mom."
We are just a bit giddy inside.

Because we know it's hard "out there" (in the big wide world).

For them. And for us.

Because we know kindness "in here" (in our safe homes and hearts) makes it a little softer.

For them. And for us.

Because in a world where flashy and shiny and costly seem to be way high on the kid list, it's the ordinary mom things, like "mom love" in a little brown bag, that are right at the top.

For them. And especially for us.

[Esther]

30
HARD THING

My kid's Hard.Thing.That.They.Are.Going.Through.

I want to control it fix it change it erase it.
I want to take it on myself so they don't have to feel it.
I want it gone.

It wrecks me that I can't.

I mean BREAKS ME APART.
TEARS ME UP LEVELS ME.

This is the worst thing for a mom who loves too-much-for-some-but-not-enough-EVER-for-her.

The smashing my heart takes when my kid is in pain.
And I can't do anything about it.

Well, sort of.

I can listen and be available.
I can shed my own needed tears.
I can hurt quietly.
I can suggest.

But I can't do the thing I want to the most.

Take it from their tired body, sling it around my shoulders, and carry it for them.

Oh how I want to.

This is motherhood.

Loving so hard that the shattering is inevitable.
And being responsible, always, for picking up the pieces.

I wouldn't wish it on anybody.
But I wouldn't trade it for anything.

[Melissa]

We should never try to change our kids, but how wonderful is it to keep planting seeds in their hearts that might just bloom one day?

MOMS OF BICS
estherjoygoetz.com

31

QUITTING

There once was a nine-year-old who asked her mom for a lacrosse stick. And goggles. And to join a cute team of other nine-year-olds.

Which meant cleats and a uniform and driving back and forth to three practices a week and God-knows-how-many games.

It made sense. Her older sister played. Her two older brothers played. Lacrosse equipment littered the garage, the kitchen, the trunk of the car and the talk around the table.

What was a mom to do?

She was exhausted with all the laundry, the cooking, the driving, the homework, the music lessons, the mayhem of motherhood.

This mom, who was awful at making good boundaries and had the illusion she was supermom, responded with "yes."

She loved sports. And who knows? "Maybe her final child had a chance at the big leagues" (whatever the heck that means when it comes to women's lacrosse).

A fancy stick was purchased.
Along with pink goggles (a two-pack) and black cleats with a pink stripe.

Forms were filled out along with a hefty check.
Practices were driven to, back and forth, back and forth, back and forth.

Cheering happened at games and mom friendships were formed on sidelines.

The little girl loved it.
So did her mom.

Year after year, the girl grew and played and grew and played.

Fancier sticks.
Bigger goggles.
Straight-up black cleats (no more pink stripe).
Special lessons.
Elite teams.

Very very soon (like a minute in mom years), the nine-year-old was donning a nylon mesh pinnie and headed to high school tryouts.

After a week of running and catching and dodging and attacking, the news came. She had made Junior Varsity.

The not-so-little girl loved it.
So did her getting-older mom.

More practices.
More driving.
More special and elite this-and-that.
More money.
More time.

News the following tryout year was even better. She had made Varsity as a lowly sophomore. Varsity.

The season was long. And hard.
The coach was rough. And knowledgeable.
The girl was in shape. And very very busy.

The big girl loved it less and less.
The couldn't-wait-for-the-next-game mom loved it more and more.

The announcement came one end-of-winter morning.

"I'm quitting lacrosse, Mom. I want to focus on my music. I want to help in the church sound booth."

This mom gathered herself quickly and tempered her aghast look (hopefully).

What was she to say?
To do?

This was not what she wanted. Or expected.
This would make her sad. Very sad.

"Okay honey. It's your life and you should do what you want with it. You do you."

That is what she said out loud.
That is what she meant down deep in her heart.
That is what she believed in her mom soul.

She wanted this girl to be completely herself and do whatever it took to find out what that was.

But her mom loss was big.

The loss of standing on the sidelines, enjoying the crisp spring air, cheering for her girl.
The loss of easy friendships she had long-formed within the lacrosse microcosm.
The loss of her expectation of what her girl might accomplish or be.

So this mom who was learning better boundaries and how to take care of herself just a little bit more, gave herself permission to be sad.

Just plain old sad. For a while.

You know what?

She still really misses all things lacrosse. Very much.
She hasn't gotten rid of the sticks. Not quite yet.

But her girl??

Her girl loves music. And sound-board buttons.
And her mom especially loves that her girl found that out.

The End. For Now.

[Esther]

32
GLITTER

She was always my magic.

A fistful of glitter tossed in the breeze. She was rainbows poured over my head, colors cascading over my skin.

She was tangled hair and unfiltered lips.

She was trees to climb and trampolines to flip on and popsicle drips on a hot summer day.

She still is.

She makes me think about the "whys" of things.

Things that have always been ONE WAY and it never occurred to me that it could be a hundred others.

She is love.

She doesn't just love the easy ones.
She loves the ones who it shouldn't make sense to love.
She doesn't ask permission from the world.
She just splits her heart open and loves until she overflows.

She is the burst of a camera flash that is so bright it makes your eyes water.

She is fingertips delicately picking up tiny creatures and placing them in safety.

She is universes and mysteries and pinkish-purple horizons barely contained by flesh and bones, spider-leg long eyelashes, and sass.

She is so HER.

So much so that she can't help teaching me to be...

...more ME.

[Melissa]

33
LET THEM LEAD

[1:00 pm, Sat]

We tried to move my son out. We rented a Uhaul, loaded up our cars and off we went out of our neighborhood, following our son in his car.

[11:00 am, Sat (two hours earlier...)]

"Want to take this pan?" I asked.
"Want this paper towel holder?" I continued.
"Want me to pack your TV in this special box?" I went on and on.

"NO."
"NO!"

and

"NO! Stop asking Mom! I've got this! And if I don't, it's on me!! I'll have to deal with it!!"

were his very firm replies.

[1:00 pm, Sat]

I tried to stop myself and did for the most part, except for sneaking a bag in my car loaded with paper plates, plasticware, toilet paper and paper towels, along with a Lysol wipes container.
Something in my mom gut just said "DO IT!"

As I followed close behind him in my overly-laden SUV, this thought struck me:

It's my job as a mom to follow his lead. Especially now! But I believe it always has been, as long as his lead is not harmful to himself or others (on purpose).

[Sometime in the early 2000s...kind-of forever ago but totally five minutes ago according to this mama]

This little guy was determined to wear matching outfits and collect Pokemon cards and take naps until he was five. He was very particular about who his friends were and didn't like anyone who was loud and bossy (which made it interesting with his loud and bossy brother).

So I learned to follow his lead.

And this particular kid taught me in spades how right that was for me as his mom, no matter his age and stage.

Like the time he, in no uncertain terms, told his dad and I to stop yelling at him to "do this or that" from the sidelines and if we didn't stop, he would just do the opposite.

"Shoot the ball!" we would yell.

And within seconds, the ball would be out of his hands, passed to his teammate and nowhere near the basket.

So I learned to follow his lead.

Our kids are not mini-mes. They are themselves.

They have thoughts and likes and opinions and dislikes and strengths and smarts and our main job as moms is to help them know themselves and in, turn, trust themselves.

It's probably one of the hardest jobs we have, because boy, oh boy, do we think we know better so often. And boy oh boy, are we trustworthy (cough, cough)!

And perhaps, we do.
Or we might.
Or we are.

But it's for them to find that out all on their own.

One of our big mom goals isn't for our kids to stay safe and secure in our nest, doing what we think is best for them mostly because it feels good to us. Our goal is for them to fly on their own, taking paths designed only for them, no matter how yucky and strange and uncomfortable it is for us.

And another of our big mom goals (or at least mine) is for us to have long-term, healthy, loving relationships with our kids when they become real-live adults! Not one where they are pestered to death with all our ideas, shutting down their own, but one where their "no" AND their "yes" are respected and their foibles and successes are theirs alone, one where we follow their lead and are there to support them when it all goes to hell in a hand-basket.

[2:30 pm, Sat]

We got to the apartment and unloaded it all, and our very determined, independent son found out he had forgotten his very important pillow, the certain kind of popcorn he loves so much and to set up the internet! And mind you, he loves video games like every other baby adult male. No internet = no video games.

[7:00 pm, Sat]

Back home he came to sleep.

[11:00 am, Sun]

He woke, shuffled upstairs and said two of my favorite things in the world:

"Mom, can you help me set up the internet?"

and

"Mom, I think I'll take that paper towel holder after alll! It's a really good match! Oh, and can you get me some salt and pepper at the store when you go tomorrow!?"

[5:00 pm, Tues]

I waved goodbye as he pulled out of our driveway, his car laden with much more than salt and pepper and a paper towel holder.

It was filled with his favorite groceries, his forgotten pillow and popcorn, and hopefully the roots of my unconditional love, tucked down deep in his heart.

[Esther]

34

GRIEVE

As much as I love being a witness to my kids' becomings,
I grieve.

I grieve the moments swallowed up by the years.

Tiny toddler hands hanging onto my pinkies.
Scared voices calling out for me in the middle of the night.

Dirt and syrup and fresh air captured in their wrinkles.
The smell of them fresh out of the tub.

Baby curls at their temples and the napes of their necks.

I grieve their need for me, that bottomless need that I could never seem to fill.

They always needed more and it exhausted me at the time, but in this moment, in the grieving moments, I crave it like drug.

Sometimes I can hear echoes of the past ringing loudly.

The infectious way they used to giggle.
A subtle expression flickering across their faces that takes me to when they were young and it is a surprise punch to the gut.

That version of them has layers of imperceptible transformations laid on top.

I want to go back for a second.
Just one.

I want to feel the weight of their heads in my lap, their tiny hands pressed into mine.

I want to swing them around in circles: once, twice, three times, to hear their giggles.

I want to hear their high-pitched voices say "Mama" and "Mommy" and "I love you."

I make space now to both adore my big kids and crave those littles.

Grief winds around my limbs, a vine I keep cutting back.

I choose to welcome the losses as they come, usher them in and ask them to sit.

We just sit for a while.

[Melissa]

35
DROPPING SHOES

This mom feeling has plagued me all my life.

It's been showing up a lot lately no matter how much I try to push it down, aside, or out the back door.

Last week, the phone rang, but it was facedown and on silent.

When I went to check it for some other reason and saw "missed call" from one of my kids, my heart went for its usual race and my palms got all sweaty.

You see, this child of mine was supposed to be somewhere doing something and now they were calling.

Not texting. Calling.

[Is your mom head nodding?]

There it was: that "wait for the shoe to drop" feeling.

Lately, we've had relative calm in our family, which just means that there hasn't been a major emergency.

But instead of leaning in and enjoying the season of mom rest, I'm on edge looking up at the sky for some giant high-heeled footwear to come stomping down on my head.

I found out it's called "foreboding joy."

There's good news and bad news about it.

BAD NEWS FIRST (because that's how I roll).

Joy is the most vulnerable emotion and we are terrified of losing it, so we actually practice tragedy. Seriously?

Everyone does it and I bet us moms do it even more. How could we not? We've all got a little mom PTSD, right?

But it comes at a high price. We find ourselves either numbing out or spinning around with anxiety. YUCK.

BUT THERE IS SOME GOOD NEWS. [phew]
And it's pretty simple. [phew]

We can replace practicing tragedy with practicing gratitude. It's kind of the key to quieting down that "shoe is going to drop" feeling. [phew] Thanks Brene Brown for that nugget of wisdom.

And believe it or not, it trains our mom brain to have more room for joy. [phew]

Joy for all that's right and good and lovely in our mom lives.
Joy in the middle of the mayhem of all the mom things.
Joy that sneaks out and reminds us, "You have permission to enjoy. Right now. Stop and take it all in."

I'm not sure what will happen the next time I miss a phone call from my baby-adults.

I might still freak out and look up and cover my head for the impending Adidas, but hopefully I won't stay there.

Perhaps I'll get an umbrella and breathe a prayer of thanks instead.

It's certainly worth a try.

[Esther]

My daughter is fierce and sassy,
hilarious and sweet. She wears
clothes she's comfortable in and
says what's on her mind and
knows what she wants.
I always dreamt I'd have a
daughter that wanted
to be like me.
It didn't occur to me that
I'd have a daughter and that
I'd want to be like her.

 NEVER EMPTY NEST

36
NOTHING DAYS

I love our Nothing Days best of all.

The days that spread out in front of us like a checkered blanket in the sand, sunshine kissing the tops of our heads, wind throwing open the conversation.

The days that we hop in the car and you take the wheel and decide where we are going. I try hard not to backseat-drive, even though I do just a bit.

To our favorite small coffee shop with plant-lined windows and local art on the walls, the barista already punching in our order before we utter a word.

To Target to try on hats and sunglasses we have no intention of buying, so you can tell me what skin care products are good and which are SO bad for me. To search for the perfect-size hoops or some ultra comfy flannel pants.

The days we just flop on your bed and watch TikToks you find hilarious that I don't get, or memes I practically pee my pants laughing at, but you find "cringey."

The Nothing Days that you are up for anything and even let me take our selfies.

And we laugh so hard at the smallest things, so hard tears stream down our cheeks and I start wheezing.

And we tell each other secrets and indulge in the latest girly gossip.

I love the times we have just an hour or two for Nothing.

A quick run to get groceries or walk our terrible-on-walks dogs or get some fast food fries.

A long talk as we lean against the kitchen counter or you bake cookies and save me a spoonful of dough (though I want to just eat it all before you bake it).

I will let the tears fall after you are out of the house and our doing Nothing together halts and stalls.

I am stock-piling those days just so I can pull them out and feel our togetherness once again.

Please know how much Nothing with you has actually been Everything to me.

It has been my favorite.

So if the mood strikes you and you feel like doing Nothing with me anytime soon again...

you should already know my answer will be...

"Do you even need to ask?!?"

[Melissa]

37
MESSES

Finding the beets upside-down in the vegetable drawer first thing in the morning, their bright red juice settled into the cracks, almost did me in.

"I'm always cleaning up messes," I grumped to my husband. "I've been doing it forever."

After pulling out the drawer, taking out the veggies, some salvageable and some crimson-stained and headed for the garbage, and using lots of those precious Lysol wipes and paper towels (I still have PTSD from those dang COVID days) every time I use them), I looped back to what I had just said.

"I'm always cleaning up messes. I've been doing it forever."

Nothing is truer for a mom.

Physical messes.

Poopy diapers that have somehow gone all the way up the back.
Legos strewn all over the family room floor.
Throw-up because of a teen's poor choice.
Dishes in sink from 20-something's midnight cooking spree.

Emotional messes.

Toddler tantrums because of God-knows-what.
Tears over mean middle school girls at lunch tables.
Hearts broken by first crushes.
Dreams shattered over college rejections.

As I plopped down on my office couch, something hit me like a ton of bricks.

What about my own messes?

The ones that I try to hide as best I can?
The kind that leak out and get all over?
The messes I don't have time for because I'm cleaning up everyone else's?

What about those?

If I cover them up, they'll still be there.
If I don't turn them right-side-up, they'll keep leaking and getting all over.
If I don't make space to clean them up (and for me in the process), they will just keep adding to the other ones I didn't clean up yet and so on and so on and so on.

So yup.

What about my own messes?
What can I do about them?

Unhide. Uncover. Do it any which way.

Tell a friend.
Say a prayer.
Write it down.

Turn them right-side up.

Get much-needed help.
Talk to a counselor.
Go on some meds.

Make space to clean them up. Whatever it takes.

I am a priority.
I have permission to take care of me and clean up my messes.
I am allowed to love myself.

So yup.

Moms are the mess cleaner-uppers.

Always have been.
Always will be.

And the most important messes we will ever clean up are our own.

[Esther]

38
SHOW UP

It's a really big deal that I show up for my kids.

My mom always shows up.
Always has.

I never have to ask. She just does.
I never have to wonder. I already know.

It doesn't matter the time of day or how far away it is or how long of a day she has had herself.

She works two jobs. Two full-time jobs.
She takes care of my dad, a recent stroke survivor.

But she still shows up for me.
And she shows up for my kids, too. Always has.

Not just big events. Little stuff.

Like dropping off Valentine's Day cards to my big kids and sending flowers to school when my daughter makes it to skiing sectionals and paying for my college kid's parking pass just because.

She shows up when I've gone to the emergency room and drops off a pizza on our wedding anniversary and buys me plants to put in my garden in the spring.

She shows up for us all.

Because momming is her life and she can't help herself and she will continue to do this forever.

Her mom was the same way.

Always taking care of her kids and grands and great-grands.

Sending cards and making birthday phone calls and flooding heaven with prayers.

I learned from the best.

My grandma showed up.
My mom shows up.
I show up.

And I have a strong feeling
my kids will be Show Ups too.

Love you, mom.
Thanks for continuing to pave the way.

[Melissa]

39
PRESENCE

The back door opens.
It's late.

I'm awake because that's just how it is as a mom. No sleep until every child of mine is home safe.

My recent college grad walks into the family room where I lay on the couch, eyes heavy.

"We broke up, Mom."

I bolt upright, dumbfounded. I can't compute the words I hear.

This boy of mine and his girlfriend have been together since they were kids.

Seven years.

Tears form in his green eyes.

I don't know what to do. I haven't seen him cry since he was little.

This is a girl he was going to propose to.
This is a girl I love. Her picture hangs on our family photo wall.

I want to fix it, make him okay.

I am sad. I am angry.
I want to send her a "please love my boy again" text.
I want to buy him a plane ticket to visit his sister.

My own eyes well up and I offer him the only thing I can: my presence.

This is how it is now. The older my kids get, what they need comforting for or help with are not things I can do much about.

I can't make people like them.
I can't (and shouldn't) fight on their behalf for a grade or a promotion at work.
I can't force someone to want to spend the rest of their lives with them.

I can't stop the world from hurting them.

What am I to do?

The only thing I can.

Offer my presence.

In simple ways.

Answer their text with a simple "I love you."
Listen when and if they want to talk.
Take them to a movie, complete with popcorn and candy.
Write a "you've got this" note.
Make their favorite cookies.
Remind them I am praying for them.

Offer my presence.

Their lives are going to be filled with problems I can't solve and pain I can't take away.

This might be the most difficult part of being a mom. But perhaps it's also the most beautiful.

I'm not doing the work that's theirs alone.
I'm not fixing the dilemmas they find themselves in.
I'm not concocting ways to ensure they are not in pain (try as I might).

I am being with them in the middle of the quagmire.
I am reminding them they are not left on their own.
I am here for them, worrying, trusting, cheering, praying and hoping.

There's no place I'd rather be.

[Esther]

40
DON'T KNOW

I don't know what I'm doing.
Did you know that, kids?

Like no idea. What I'm doing.
None.

I was terrified to bring you home from the hospital.

Afraid I wouldn't know what to do with you. Overwhelmed at the prospect of having to keep a tiny little creature that I helped make alive and breathing and safe and happy.

I've never stopped being afraid all these years later.
I've never stopped worrying that I was going to colossally mess you up.

Did I?
Did I mess you up?

I think I have loved you as much as a mother possibly can.

I don't think I kept an inch of my heart for myself.
I gave it all.

Can you see all that love spread out over your lives?

A patchwork quilt of kisses goodnight and hugs in the morning, holding hands across the street, quizzing you for tests, smoothing your hair back and cuddles when you were sick, making cookies and watching America's Funniest Videos and going on rides at the waterpark and laughing long into the night.

I see all the versions of you both, carried quietly in your big bodies, whispers of who you were escaping sometimes in your giggles or a fleeting expression passing like a shadow over your face.

My beautiful ones.

I don't know what I'm doing.

Did I do right by you?
Did you feel loved enough always?

I pray you know.
You are so loved.
I can't believe I get to be your mom
forever.

[Melissa]

There's no sweeter
thing at the end of a
long day than a text
from your big kid saying
"love you mom"
(if they are far away or
just down the hall).

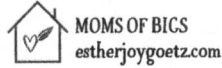

MOMS OF BICS
estherjoygoetz.com

41

TWINGE

It hits you when you least expect it.
That **TWINGE** of mom grief.

The lump in your throat, tear in your eye, and melancholy in your mom heart.

It might be something as simple as...

watching your 10-year-old jump in a pile of leaves knowing this might be the last time she feels carefree enough to do so because she is heading into those self-conscious middle school years.

TWINGE.

Or...

your eighth grader asking to stand back-to-back with you so he can prove he has passed you up in the mom/son height race.

TWINGE.

Maybe even...

your newly-licensed driver waving goodbye to you as she backs down your driveway headed off for the very first time **EVER** alone in the family car.

TWINGE.

How about...

unthinkingly grabbing your son's favorite cereal in the grocery store a week into his college freshman year? You slowly put it back on the shelf.

TWINGE.

It happened to me. Again. A sign on the beach I frequent often, one I had never noticed before.

A simple board with words reminding me that I am here, standing 428 feet from the Atlantic Ocean and my 21-year-old is snug as a bug 30 minutes from the Pacific Ocean, almost 3,000 miles away.

3,000.

TWINGE.
TWINGE.
TWINGE.

I stopped.
I stared at the sign.
I sighed.
I teared up.
I wiped my eyes with my shirt.

TWINGE.

That ever-so familiar TWINGE that...

...sparks gratitude for this mom journey I love.
...moves me THROUGH the hard of missing all the good that once was
...takes me TO the good that still lies ahead, waiting for me to enjoy it.

It won't be long until I feel that TWINGE again.

It will hit me when I least expect it.
But I secretly don't mind it at all.

[Esther]

42
THE DRESS

The dress didn't come.

The super cute one my daughter ordered online that was supposed to be here.

Today.

For her formal.
Tonight.

Didn't. Come.

What happened?

We were left with an hour and half today to find the perfect dress. Undergarments. Tights. Fake nails. Sparkly makeup. Shoes. Jewelry.

90 minutes. No more.

We rushed from store to store.
We frantically searched for her size, a size not easy to find.

We were discombobulated, frenzied, but determined.

We half-jogged through the mall, weaving expertly around elderly mall-walkers and tiny teetering tots.

We completed the mission with ten minutes to spare.
All of it, down to the tiniest details.

This is what we do for our kids.
Our people.

We take on the impossible.
We make it work.
We move heaven and earth to get the job done.

Whatever they need.

What is a big deal for them is a big deal to us.

All the sweating and the stress and the craziness is nothing compared to the smiles we get to see on their faces when it all comes together and we get to take all the pictures and see the sparkle in their eyes and bear witness to their absolute

RADIANCE.

[Melissa]

43
CAR ACCIDENT FUND

"Please do not drive around in this. There are trees down everywhere. And please do not take your younger brother with you."

Those were the words I pleaded with my new driver in a hurricane aftermath.

As you might guess, curiosity got the best of him and this "I-am-trying-hard-not-to-control-you-anymore" mama said a prayer as she watched her boys skip out the door and drive away.

Needing a few groceries since we were "out of food" (#alwayshungryteens), I ventured out to the store, gingerly driving around downed branches and wires hanging precariously, wondering if I should have taken my own advice.

On my way back to the car, grocery shopping done, my phone rang.

It was Son One.

"Mom, I got in an accident."

After saying some not-so-kind things and yelling (just a little) that this was "the exact reason" I didn't want him going out, I remembered to ask this question, "Are you okay? Is your brother okay?"

He sighed. "Yes, Mom." [PHEW]
"But..."

"...my car is not."

Now came the hard part.

How could I get him (and his tag-along brother)? They were more than 10 miles away.

After calling the tow service, I instructed my boys to find a safe(ish) place on the side of the road, far away from all scary wires and dangling branches.

Over two hours later, groceries wilting and melting, my mama heart determined to reach her boys (still a little bit angry, I might add), I arrived on the scene.

There they sat, their over six-foot-tall crumpled bodies, heads down, on the grassy slope aside a busy intersection in a strange town.

In that moment, instead of two giant almost-men who had "defied" my very sound mom advice, I saw my two little boys, needing their mom.

Not needing her to yell.
Not needing her to say "I told you so."
Not needing her to tell them they were "going to reap the consequences" and that "I was not going to pay a dime for the car to be fixed."

Just needing their mom.

Needing her to scoop them up.
Needing her to show them grace.
Needing her to drive them home, their safest space of all.

Safe to make choices.
Safe to make mistakes.
Safe to make "the call."

After watching the tow truck load his car and following it carefully along the tree-branch-riddled roads, we finally made it home in one piece, my usually very chatty new driver quiet the whole way.

As we came inside, he headed right into the kitchen and found an old jar and wrote "Car Accident Fund" in sharpie on the outside and placed it on the dining room table.

What did I do?

I got out my wallet and stuck a few bills in there immediately.

He smiled.

So did I.

[Esther]

44
SENIOR

When you're the mom of a high school senior...

Your momma heart is FULL UP on grief.
Counting down all the lasts.

Trying to freeze time.
Or better yet, travel back in time.

It's painful to think about 18 years getting wrapped up neatly with a graduation bow.
Like, how does a mother even DO THAT?

You'll be flooded with memories and I Wish I Hads and Did I Do Enoughs.

You'll feel guilty for trying to hang on to all the versions of your baby with a death grip.
And how terrified you are of loosening that grip.

But right now, you don't have to let go just yet.
You're allowed to feel it all.

Take your baby in.
Soak 'em up.
Laugh and cry and reminisce.

There will be a time, several steps from now, that you will have to relax your hands and release your baby adult.

But you don't have to get ahead of yourself.

You have this moment now.

Wrap your baby in a hug.
Take pictures.
Listen to the laughter.
Feel the anticipation.
Let your breath be snatched by how who THAT CHILD has become.

Marvel.
Cherish.
And FEEL IT.

This transformation is a big one.
And it only gets better.

It. Only. Gets. Better.

You can do this.

Love and hugs from a mom who's been there and who's doing it again.

Right alongside of you.

[Melissa]

45
HERS
___

Once upon a time there was a mom who was struggling with her own mom.

It all started when she became a mom and wanted to be different than her mom.

In fact, she made a vow once she saw her filled-with-baby belly to do motherhood so much differently.

Her mom had worked.
She wanted to stay home.

Her mom had often been a curator of guilt.
She never wanted to do that (even though it still happened).

Her mom had sent her (and her brothers) to boarding school so she could do big things for God.
She wanted to spend every night tucking her kids into their own beds right down the hall.

Her mom struggled with listening, had talked a lot, often turning the discussion back to her.
She wanted to (she still a hard time with this) listen and give space for everyone in the conversation.

As time marched on, the struggle didn't get better. It got worse.

So she went for help. From a professional, mind you.

She learned to make boundaries.

Sometimes they were easy. But most times, they were not.

In fact, oftentimes, they were violated and that guilt (like it had when she was a girl) came pouring in.

She learned that she was allowed to be her very own person, doing the mom thing her very own way.

That was really hard.

To be a responsible mom, she had to be a disobedient daughter.

She wishes she could say that it all got better and the story ended in a happily ever after.

But that isn't the truth.
The struggle is still with her all the time.

The boundaries have had to get stronger and harder.
She's had to draw some "don't-ever-cross-this" lines.
And she's had to say things she never ever wanted to say.

It's been very sad for her.
She's bothered by it a lot.
But she's sticking with it.

And the very very good news is that she has been and still is able to do her mom thing the way she imagined (for the most part) and it's very very different.

It's not perfect.
But it feels better.
And in the end, it's hers.

And hers alone.

[Esther]

I absolutely adore my big kids. But there are times I miss their littleness with a force that steals the breath out of my lungs.

 NEVER EMPTY NEST

46
SLEEPLESS

My daughter came into our bedroom with a discombobulated messy bun and distress etched in her eyes.

"I was panicking last night and couldn't sleep. I only slept an hour," she whispered dejectedly.

"Come here, baby," I sitting up and enveloping her in a tight hug.

I gave her the option to say home from school and do class online. Thankfully right now that's possible.

It's the third time in three weeks she's stayed home due to insomnia.

I know the condition all too well.

As a child, I had crippling anxiety. At the time, of course, I didn't know what it was. All I knew was that I couldn't sleep. In fact, bedtime was my least favorite part of the day.

My mind spun like a top the second my head touched the pillow. Hours upon hours of running scenarios.

Afraid of burglars breaking into the house or a fire starting or ghosts.

I would re-live past conversations.

I would worry about upcoming tests, getting picked last in gym, or forgetting my locker combination.

I would stress about being left out of friend gatherings, or worse yet, getting invited.

I had an unnerving fear of sleepovers because I knew I wouldn't be sleeping. At all.

When my daughter was little and would wake in the middle of the night, she would get up, turn her bedtime CD back on, and quickly drift back into a deep sleep.

She always slept hard. An earthquake couldn't stir her.

I wish there was a simple fix now. A magical playlist that could erase her worries and ease the panic. There is no lullaby that powerful.

I remember the insomnia that plagued me: lying in bed for hours, exhausted but so restless, the numbers on the clock forever changing, speeding up, mocking me.

Having to go to school with dull gray cobwebs draped in my brain. My bones weeping from fatigue.

I told no one about my sleeplessness nor my anxiety.
I lived with it alone. No, suffered with it alone.

I am grateful my daughter doesn't have to.

I can't take this burden from her. But I can understand. I can listen. I can wrap her in my embrace and give her the day off of school.

I wish I could do more but that has to be enough.

And for as long as she'll let me, I will be her stand-in lullaby.

[Melissa]

47
FIXING

When I mess up as a mom, I tell myself I won't do it again.

Welp, I did it again.

It all started on a beautiful day with my big.

Everything was going along swimmingly until...

the dreaded shock came.

Something she worked hard on for a month had been destroyed over night.

Something she put her heart into.
Something she was proud of.

GONE.

She sat down in the middle of the mess and started to sob.

I stood right there taking it all in.

I began on the good, loving empathy path.

"I'm sorry honey. That's just horrible."

I knew I should let her cry.

But very quickly, when she didn't "get over it" fast enough for my liking, I moved into the place I swore I would never go again.

"It is what it is."
"We can fix this."
"At least..."

It gets worse.

I left to get something to fix it.

Just like that.

Not long later, with the BIG FIX in hand, I shouted "I have a surprise for you!"

There she sat with mascara-stained cheeks.

"I just wanted to be upset, Mom. No fixing."

I took her in at that moment. I couldn't believe that even though I knew better, I still didn't do better.

"I'm sorry," I finally said, tears welling. "I'm sorry I wanted to rush you through your grief before you were ready."

You know what happened?

I wish I could tell you that we hugged and she was fine and there was some magical immediate healing.

BUT...NOPE.

It didn't get fixed. As I write this, she still feels very upset. She should. It was a huge loss.

The good news is that I'm not beating myself to a mental pulp. There are times when even though I "know better," I still don't "do better." I'm still shocked, but have moved to a place of grace and space for my imperfect humanness.

Because that's just how it is as a mom.

We take steps forward, sideways, backward and forward again.

We press in and press on.
We mess up and fess up.
We learn more and love better (or worse and then better again).

I had to leave my sweet girl soon after the screw up.

But tonight, I got a text, delicious icing on a very bad-tasting cake.

"I was sad that the whole thing interrupted our morning together, but I wasn't ready to move to joy. I love you Mom."

[Esther]

48
LIMIT

I can't take my eyes off a photo of my daughter and me.
She was years younger than she is now.

Still on her phone. Yes.

I was relieved in that photograph moment that I still had time.

Time for first dances and more crushes and more seasons of her competing in her sport and going to homecomings and for her to fall in love with coffee.

Time for hugs before bed and for her to get tired of saying "I love you."

Time for Halloweens where she still dressed up, even if she felt too old. Time for Christmas stockings and Easter baskets and pretending she wasn't outgrowing those things.

Time. Not limitless, but more.

Now there is much less. There is definitely a limit.
And I am counting every day with her.

It came faster than I ever imagined.
So breathtakingly, heart-wrenchingly quick.

I breathe her in when she pauses next to me long enough.
I stare too long. I stuff snippets of her--memories, notes, smiles--in my pockets.

I linger in her doorway trying to commit this 17-year old face to memory.

I am grieving her leaving in a year, even though she is right in front of me.

I am jealous of photo me, Me Then, with all those years still spread out in front of us.

[Melissa]

49
GOODBYES AND HELLOS

I'm awake. It's 4 a.m. Just 45 minutes ago, I heard the garage door open and close for the last time at this ungodly hour. I ran downstairs to give and get a hug from our youngest.

You see, tonight was the night of nights. After a final dinner celebrating our two graduates, my baby and her best friend did what they always do. They drove around enjoying our sleepy little town and the surrounding area, talking about all those things BFFs talk about.

This was their last time to do that as neighbors who've known each other (and been mostly inseparable) since they were just six years old.

I don't blame them.
It's really hard to say goodbye.

After hugging and crying when she came in, and clinging to her (and secretly wishing I never had to let go), she went to sleep in her childhood bed for one more dreamy night. I tried to venture back into my own fitful sleep, but gave up as swirling emotions coursed through the bones of my soul.

You see, today is the day of days. I begin the long goodbye of driving my precious baby girl across the country to her new life on the other coast in Burbank, California. 2,764 miles from our house to her new apartment.

That's really far.
We leave in just 11 hours.

When she burst on the scene 19 years, 10 months ago, I never fathomed the ache I would hold in my heart this morning. The proud and painful and thankful and joyful and awful ache.

It's the universal mom ache that comes every time we say goodbye.

It starts when our babies take their first toddling and tentative steps away from us. That initial ache comes unbidden as we grasp a glimpse of all the future steps they will take away from us, all the goodbyes to come.

The goodbye of walking onto a school bus or into a classroom for the very first time. Tiny hands turn and wave. The ache rears and settles.

The goodbye of a first sleepover or summer camp. They are not "right in the next room," safe under the cover of our home. The ache rears quietly and settles quickly.

The goodbye of their very independent, "I've got this," preteen self. This one smacks loud and jolts abruptly. The ache rears ferociously and settles slowly.

The goodbye of a challenging teen mishap. Their childhood innocence door slams shut. The ache rears dragging fear along with it and settles in fits and starts.

The goodbye of backing out of the driveway moments after receiving freedom in the shape of a gift from the Division of Motor Vehicles. This ache rears with memories of a toddler in her car seat and settles with some much-needed freedom from late-night, seemingly endless pickups.

The goodbye of a graduation cap and a college dorm room. Stopping here for a moment. This one was really rough for me. This ache rears and settles, rears and settles, rears and settles, every time they come home and leave, come home and leave, come home and leave.

The goodbye I find myself in this morning. The goodbye of moving out and moving on. The goodbye that speaks to adulthood, active parenting job done, "will they make it on their own?

This ache rears fresh and raw this morning.
I am hopeful it will settle.

There are more goodbyes to come. The goodbye of weddings and births of grandchildren.

Every time, the steps are further and further away.
Every time, the ache rears and rears and rears
Every time, the ache settles and settles and settles.

I know that with each goodbye comes a settling hello. A settling hello that brings newness, possibility and life. Believe me, I know.

But in the wee hours of this morning, I sit in the real, raw ache of the goodbye, not rushing the pride I feel, the pain I feel, the thankfulness I feel, the joy I feel and the awfulness I feel.

It's beautiful here.
It's sacred here.
It's momentous here.

The sun is not up yet. I sit quiet in the dark. The ache will settle soon enough and the hello will come.

But I like the ache for now.
It's my very good friend.

[Esther]

50
MORE TIME

Drag me out of this season, because I don't want to go.

This particular season with my big kids has me holding on with every cell in my body. I can't let go.

I want to.
Desperately.

I want to dive head first into the next chapter, so hard my head hits the bottom and I get a concussion.
I want to see stars.

But I can't. I am trapped in transition.
Mom purgatory.

I want to open the windows and flush out the scents of this season. The fragrance of it has soaked the walls.

There is a empty room I walk by a hundred times a day and I weep.

A hundred times a day.

Put the memories back on the shelves please. Leave them alone. Let them collect dust. Don't pack them away.

There is an open spot where a car should be, but it's not taking up valuable space that the neighbors covet anymore. It's available for anyone to occupy.

But I don't want just anyone.
I want my baby.

I am sad a million different ways and I feel sideways and inside out.

My heart hangs.

I just want what I can't have.

More time.

[Melissa]

I want to be the
reason my kids
can say,
"I felt loved today."

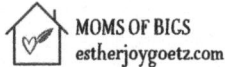

MOMS OF BIGS
estherjoygoetz.com

ACKNOWLEDGEMENTS

ESTHER'S THANKS

Without the people who call me mom and have given me blanket permission to write all our intertwined, crazy stories, this book would still be wordless memories stuck inside of me. I am so grateful to you, Sarah, Jared, Josh and Rachel, for healing my heart in unimaginable ways and allowing me to put pen to paper.

To my MOBKST writer's group who believes in me, you are what makes my words go round and round, literally. And to Her View From Home, for sharing my first words with the world. Thank you. I've learned so much from all of you.

To all my friends that just get me and build me up, listen to my crazy life and tell me I still belong to you, I wouldn't be able to do this without you: my Spice Girls, my Beautiful Mess, my Rewilders and my Sanctuary, plus ALL my long-time phone-a-friends. My heart is full.

To Melissa, seriously? We get to do this thing together? YAY!

A special shout-out to Brittany Meng, who helped me with the down-and-dirty details of getting this out into the world.

Thank you so much to my Moms of Bigs social media community for asking for this over and over again and cheering for me relentlessly as I actually made this happen.

And lastly, to Allen, the one who spoke the words, "I will be here till death do us part" so long ago, the one who has been my confidant and my support, the one who said, "your voice needs to be heard," I don't know what I'd do without you. You are the best empty-nest partner a girl could have. I want to have lots and lots more chapters with you.

MELISSA'S THANKS

I can think of no greater love story than the story we create in the ordinary days with the ones we love the most. The ones who see us at our ugliest and our most glorious and everything in the mediocre middle.

Thank you to the ones who make up my love story. To my husband, Jason, for being the witness to my life, my best friend, my adventure partner, and the one who gets to take care of me when my hearing and memory fail. Lucky you! To my Griffin and Kira, the inspiration for my writing. You truly are the reason for all of it. Being your mom is the greatest and most humbling thing I get to do.

To my parents, siblings, and dear friends for your wild, unwavering support of everything I do. You show up, you celebrate, you cheer loudly. Thanks for always being in my corner.

To Carol, for making me laugh and cry and feel seen every day. I can't wait to see where life takes us next.

To my MOBKST writer friends, I truly would not be here doing all of this if it weren't for you. You are my kindreds. You get it.

To Leslie Means and Her View From Home, I am so grateful you put my words out there first. What an honor.

To Esther, I still can't believe we get to share our stories together in such an exquisite way. It was meant to be.

Finally, to my Never Empty Nest community. This collection is for you. You are the best corner of the internet and I'm beyond thankful to share this with you.

Love you all.

NOT THE END

NOT THE END